# Does TECHNOLOGY Make People Lazy?

By Katie Kawa

**KidHaven** PUBLISHING

Published in 2019 by
**KidHaven Publishing, an Imprint of Greenhaven Publishing, LLC**
353 3rd Avenue
Suite 255
New York, NY 10010

Designer: Deanna Paternostro
Editor: Katie Kawa

Photo credits: Cover Zivica Kerkez/Shutterstock.com; p. 5 (top) Rawpixel.com/Shutterstock.com; p. 5 (bottom) Twin Design/Shutterstock.com; p. 7 Olesya Kuznetsova/Shutterstock.com; pp. 9 (top), 21 (inset, middle-left) wakebreakmedia/Shutterstock.com; pp. 9 (bottom), 21 (inset, right) stockfour/Shutterstock.com; p. 11 NurPhoto/Contributor/NurPhoto/Getty Images; p. 13 Alexander Kirch/Shutterstock.com; p. 15 MJTH/Shutterstock.com; p. 17 (top) Jacob Lund/Shutterstock.com; p. 17 (bottom) Albina Tiplyashina/Shutterstock.com; p. 19 (top) AlesiaKan/Shutterstock.com; p. 19 (bottom) Xubayr Mayo/Shutterstock.com; p. 21 (notepad) ESB Professional/Shutterstock.com; p. 21 (markers) Kucher Serhii/Shutterstock.com; p. 21 (photo frame) FARBAI/iStock/Thinkstock; p. 21 (inset, left and middle-right) Monkey Business Images/Shutterstock.com.

**Cataloging-in-Publication Data**

Names: Kawa, Katie.
Title: Does technology make people lazy? / Katie Kawa.
Description: New York : KidHaven Publishing, 2019. | Series: Points of view | Includes glossary and index.
Identifiers: ISBN 9781534525641 (pbk.) | 9781534525634 (library bound) | ISBN 9781534525658 (6 pack) | ISBN 9781534525665 (ebook)
Subjects: LCSH: Technology–Social aspects–Juvenile literature. | Technology–Psychological aspects--Juvenile literature.
Classification: LCC T14.5 K379 2019 | DDC 303.48'3–dc23

Printed in the United States of America

CPSIA compliance information: Batch #BS18KL: For further information contact Greenhaven Publishing LLC, New York, New York at 1-844-317-7404.

Please visit our website, www.greenhavenpublishing.com. For a free color catalog of all our high-quality books, call toll free 1-844-317-7404 or fax 1-844-317-7405.

# CONTENTS

Two Views of Technology 4

Today's Technology 6

Too Easy? 8

Doing More to Help Others 10

Making Machines Do It All 12

Productive People 14

Filling the Free Time 16

Laziness Is a Choice 18

Breaking Down Both Sides 20

Glossary 22

For More Information 23

Index 24

# Two Views of
# TECHNOLOGY

What do the wheel and the smartphone have in common? Both are inventions that made people's lives easier. Throughout history, important advances been made made to technology, which is the method of using science to **solve** problems and the tools used to solve those problems.

Many people think new technology is helpful. However, others argue that technology can make people's lives too easy. They believe people become lazy because they can use new inventions to do things for them. People on both sides of this **debate** about technology back up their point of view with different facts.

**Know the Facts!**

As of 2015, 92 percent of teenagers in the United States go online every day.

People have strong opinions about technology. Some think it's helpful, while others think it's harmful. It's good to learn all the facts about this issue before you form your own opinion.

# Today's
# TECHNOLOGY

Technology has changed over time. Things we now think of as basic parts of life, such as paper, roads, and light bulbs, were once major advances in technology.

Today, one of the most important technological advancements used to make people's lives easier is the internet. People can go online in more ways now than ever before, including on their computers, smartphones, tablets, and even televisions. These **devices** allow people to have a large amount of **information** at their fingertips, which can be used to do work or to waste time.

## Know the Facts!

As of 2017, the average age of an American child when they got their first smartphone was 10 years old.

Smartphones are an important piece of technology, but people have different opinions about how old children should be before they get one. Some people worry that having a smartphone will make a child less active.

# Too EASY?

The internet has allowed people to quickly and easily find large amounts of information about almost any subject they can imagine. This can be very helpful, but some people believe the internet is doing too much work for people.

Before the internet, it was hard to find information. People had to read many books and newspapers to find the same number of facts they can find on one website today. Because people don't have to work as hard to find information, the internet is sometimes blamed for making people lazy.

### Know the Facts!

The Google effect is the idea that people don't have to remember as much information anymore because they can look up anything they need to know online.

The internet has changed the way people learn and remember information. Some people believe this has made our brains lazier.

9

# Doing More to Help
# OTHERS

The internet has made it easier to get information than it was in the past, but not everyone sees that as a bad thing. Many people are using the information they find online to do more work—not less.

By using technology to do things more easily and quickly, people can do more to help those who need it. For example, people use the internet to raise money and awareness for important causes. Having more information and more free time to use that information allows many people to do more good than they could have before the internet.

## Know the Facts!

As of 2016, 77 percent of Americans said they like having so much information available to them because of the internet.

Technology has helped people become more active in reporting what's going on in the world around them. Some people use their smartphones to make and share videos or news reports.

# Making Machines
# DO IT ALL

New technology isn't just being used to get information more easily, it's also being used to do basic tasks more easily. Some devices can now do tasks people once had to do themselves, such as turning on and off lights, changing radio stations, and even cleaning floors!

Some people believe **automated** inventions make people lazier because the work they once had to do can now be done by machines. This means they don't have to get up to do something as simple as turning on a light. They can now do this just by using their voice.

## Know the Facts!

A smart home is a home that has automated lights, heat, and **electronic** devices such as televisions that can all be controlled by a smartphone or computer.

Some people see smart houses, which have many automated parts, as a sign of progress. Others see them as a sign of laziness.

# Productive
# PEOPLE

Although some people believe automated devices lead to laziness, others see these inventions differently. They believe automated devices save people time, and people can use this time to do more tasks that they might not have had time to do before. Automated devices can help people become more productive, or able to do a large amount of work.

Technology can help people be more productive in other ways, too. Smartphones, smartwatches, and other devices can help people plan their days to get more work done. They can even remind people to keep moving and stay active.

## Know the Facts!

A major study of how Americans feel about technology was done in 2014. This study showed that 59 percent of Americans believe technological advancements will lead to a better future.

Many people use technology to help them stay **organized** and productive at work.

# Filling the Free
# TIME

When people have more free time because of automated technology, they sometimes use that time to be more productive. In other cases, though, they use their new free time to watch television shows, play games, or look at **social media** websites. Many people see these activities as wasting time.

When people use their free time this way, they're also generally staying in one place. This has led many people to believe technology is making people less active. When people are less active, they're more likely to become obese, or very overweight. This can lead to many health problems.

### Know the Facts!

A 2017 study showed that teenagers who spend more than five hours a day on smartphones, computers, or other devices are more likely to become obese than teenagers who spend less time using this kind of technology.

16

Technology can distract adults and kids and keep them from doing work or being **physically** active.

# Laziness Is

# A CHOICE

Many people throughout history have argued that new inventions and technology would make people lazier. Others have argued that technology might make it easier for people to be lazy if they want to be, but that doesn't mean it makes them lazy.

These people believe laziness is a choice, and new inventions can't cause people to choose to be lazy. People have to decide to be active—or inactive—on their own. Technology can be used to help people become more productive or to help them waste more time. It can't make people decide to do one or the other.

Some people believe technology can be used to help people work harder or help them find new ways to be lazy. It's up to each person to decide how to use it.

# Breaking Down Both
# SIDES

Inventors often want to make life easier for people. Today's devices do this by keeping people more connected to each other and to news they might not have known without the internet. They also sometimes do the work people once had to do themselves, such as putting events on a calendar or parking a car.

Some people believe these advances in technology have changed people's lives for the better and have helped people become more productive. Others believe they're making people lazier and doing more harm than good. After learning about both points of view, what do you think?

## Know the Facts!

As stated in a 2015 report, American children ages 8 to 18 years old spend an average of more than 6 hours a day in front of some kind of screen, such as a smartphone or television, for fun.

# Does technology make people lazy?

## YES

- People no longer have to work to get or remember information because the internet provides it for them.

- Smartphones and other devices organize things and do tasks for people that they used to have to do themselves.

- People can waste hours of time using technology in ways that aren't productive.

- Technology allows people to be physically inactive and to do things with less effort.

## NO

- People have more information than ever and are using that information to make the world a better place.

- Technology gives people more time to do more tasks.

- Technology makes people more productive because they're constantly connected to tasks they need to do.

- Technology can't make someone lazy. They have to choose to be lazy on their own.

After looking at the arguments on both sides of this debate, do you think technology makes people lazy? What facts can you use to support your point of view?

# GLOSSARY

**automated:** Done using machines instead of people.

**debate:** An argument or discussion about an issue, generally between two sides.

**device:** A tool used for a certain purpose.

**electronic:** Operating through the use of many small electrical parts.

**information:** Knowledge or facts about something.

**organized:** Neat and orderly.

**physical:** Relating to the body.

**social media:** A collection of websites and applications, or apps, that allow users to interact with each other and create online communities.

**solve:** To find an answer or a way to deal with a problem.

# For More
# INFORMATION

## WEBSITES

**"Safe Cyberspace Surfing"**
*kidshealth.org/en/kids/internet-safety.html*
This article from the KidsHealth website offers important tips on staying safe when using the internet.

**Screen Time vs. Lean Time**
*www.cdc.gov/nccdphp/dch/multimedia/infographics/getmoving.htm*
This website provides information about how much time kids ages 8 to 10 years old spend in front of screens and what they can do instead.

## BOOKS

Blakemore, Megan. *All About Smart Technology*. Lake Elmo, MN: Focus Readers, 2017.

Hubbard, Ben. *Using Digital Technology*. Chicago, IL: Capstone, 2017.

Nagelhout, Ryan. *Freaky Stories About Technology*. New York, NY: Gareth Stevens Publishing, 2017.

# INDEX

**A**

automated inventions, 12

**B**

books, 8

**C**

computers, 6, 12, 16

**D**

devices, 6, 12, 14, 16, 20, 21

**G**

Google effect, 8

**H**

health problems, 16

**I**

important causes, 10
inactive, 18, 21
internet, 6, 8, 9, 10, 20, 21

**N**

newspapers, 8

**O**

obese, 16

**P**

productive, 14, 15, 16, 18, 20, 21

**S**

smart homes, 12
smartphones, 4, 6, 7, 11, 12, 14, 16, 20, 21
smartwatches, 14
social media, 16

**T**

tablets, 6, 18
television, 6, 12, 16, 20
time, 6, 10, 14, 16, 18, 21